VOICES
OF THE
AVALONIAN
PRIESTESSES

*Hearing the Call
of Essence*

FLOWER *of* LIFE PRESS

FLOWER *of* LIFE PRESS

Cover art and interior art by S. Pauline Michalovic, infinitehealth@miraclewrx.com

Cover and book design by Jane Astara Ashley, www.floweroflifepress.com

Published by Flower of Life Press, Old Saybrook, CT., www.floweroflifepress.com

Library of Congress Control Number: Available upon request.
ISBN-13: 978-1-7349730-0-6
Printed in the United States of America

Contents

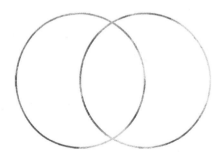

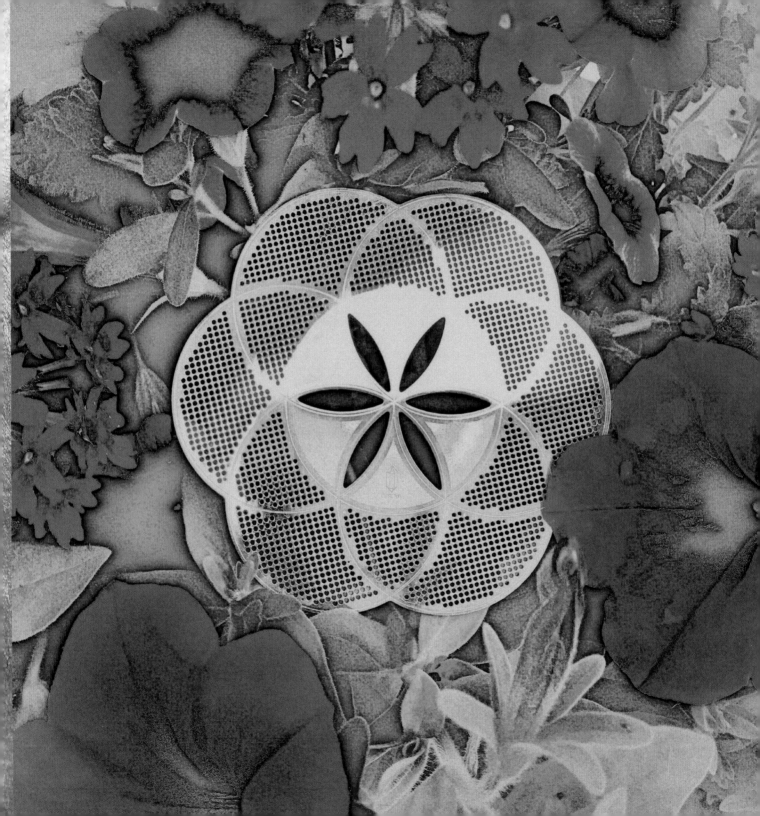

Note from the Editor

By Rebecca Cavender

In 2017, the temple was entering its second year of teaching the intensive, year-long priestess training, Enter the Mystery.

Many sisters were re-enrolling and there was the desire to create a deepening track so they could focus on—in addition to the regular "curriculum"—specific priestess tools and skills. Most of the returning women indicated they wanted to learn more about sacred, intuitive writing.

Women also wanted to learn more about sacred geometry, mudras and mantras, and the sacred tool for each of the 13 Divine Feminine archetypes studied in Enter the Mystery. With this in mind, the temple created a "Sacred Tools" tract allowing women to deepen with all of these priestess skills.

As the copywriter, scribe, and oracle of the Priestess Presence Temple, and a senior priestess, I was asked, as part of my personal devotion and training, if I'd be willing to create a 12 month Sacred Writing track within the Sacred Tools—Enter the Mystery program.

It was an honor and blessing to create a year-long curriculum to support women to truly learning how to listen deeply within and be a vessel so they can write transmissions from the Divine Feminine.

Part of the training included understanding that when you're learning to write as though it is a sacred tool, you become an oracle. A channel. A vessel of the divine, ultimately embodying and transmitting divine feminine archetypal energies. This is a responsibility and requires becoming adept in discernment so that you can feel whether the message you're channeling is aligned, true, and in service to the collective. Their training included:

- A Sacred Writing manual
- Crystalline-Diamond Light Body Activation (The Heart Center of Crystalline Truth™)
- Monthly worksheets with written instructions to practice writing transmissions for each specific divine feminine archetype
- Audio journey and intuitive writing prompt

- Several live, online writing circles to practice their skills
- Personal 1:1 activation of their True Voice—their sacred self-expression

At the end of the year, they were offered the opportunity to submit their sacred writing for the book, *Voices of the Avalonian Priestesses.*

This book is a collection of their dedication to begin accessing writing as a sacred tool, in devotion to the Goddess.

Sisters learned the power of words, their ability to heal, to transmit truth, and amplify love. My hope was that by learning to become a clear vessel, they'd have an embodied experience of feeling connected to themselves, the Goddess, and all living things; this provides the gift of an imprinted knowing that we are all whole and simultaneously part of one another.

This is medicine. Medicine that you now hold in your hands.

We are in a time where it is now safe to express our love of the Goddess and openly be in service to Her, yet this takes courage. I honor this courage in each one of the priestesses who contributed to the book.

Thank you for your depth and willingness to share Her voice as it is expressed through you.

~A NOTE OF THANKS TO JULIA CASCIOLA~

One of the temple's priestesses, Julia Casciola, significantly supported me in the editorial process of this book. Her highly attuned heart and sensitive discernment with words and their frequency helped us to ensure that the essential truth of the transmissions were cut through and brought forth as clearly as possible.

This sometimes means honing a metaphorical crystallized sword that can slice apart words that come from the mind and adeptly focus on those that have the energy of the Goddess's breath. I am deeply grateful for Julia's precision, discernment, and devotion to the temple.

Introduction

~HEARING THE CALL OF ESSENCE~

By Elayne Kalila Doughty

Beloved One,

We welcome you here into the heart of our Priestess Presence temple… for this is where you stand.

Imagine that you are being greeted at the temple door by a sister who is dressed in a long sapphire blue robe, with a moonstone at her heart. As you look into her eyes you are brought into an eternal now moment and enveloped in timelessness...

As you enter into this temple you are embraced by a circle of sisters who have been awaiting you—they anoint your hands and feet with the delicious scent of roses and welcome you into their midst. They bring you hot tea and place you on a comfy couch. And then they lovingly offer you this book as a welcome gift...

What lies between the covers of this book is an invitation into remembrance—to slow down and stop for a moment to listen into your heart, and to receive the hearts and souls of a circle of women who have taken the Priestess Initiation journey to remember the Essence of who they are…

Each sister who shares in this beautiful book has been on a journey of deep healing into wholeness within the Enter the Mystery Priestess Initiate Circle—a profound initiation journey (founded on the 13 Moon Mystery School) to "Remember the Essence of who they truly are".

WHAT IS ESSENCE?

Your Essence is your core expression, your frequency, your unique energy. Remembering the essence of who you are is the mission of the Priestess Presence temple. Accessing this is a life-long journey of practicing consciousness skills that help you listen to and trust your inner wisdom. This is the training that the sisters who are featured in this book have committed themselves to.

Each piece in this book is a unique heart offering that was written through a process of deep listening and connection to their own Essence voice—the aspect of themselves that is eternal, that is mythic—the voice that holds the story and journey of their soul being.

So, for this reason, there are poems, paintings, photographs, artwork and short stories that are all offered from the author's hearts, as an invitation for you to more deeply connect with your Essence… and enter into a fuller remembrance of who you truly are…

As you enter into each one of these offerings your own remembrance may be awakened within you…

WHAT DOES IT MEAN TO "REMEMBER"?

Remembrance is a full sensory experience. You can feel it and communicate it through all channels of perception.

When you see an image that sparks something within you, hear a piece of music and you know how to play it or dance it, find yourself being transported to a different place while making love, smell a scent that brings tears to your eyes... without any conscious knowledge of why... you are remembering.

There is a beautiful mystery in remembrance because as much as we try to quantify it and understand it through science and logic, we cannot.

Remembrance is poetic. Mythic.

It is felt in our bodies. It is unlocked in moments of surrender and release. It is during these times that we allow ourselves to move between the veils.

On the Priestess Path, we are invited into the possibility that we can access memories of not just the past but also the future; we do not live in the confines of a time-space continuum. Memory is not anchored to times gone past.

It's a paradox that when we are fully present in a moment, we can remember. It is in this place we connect with our ancient-future self and all of its vast possibilities for the present.

Yes, we can remember other lifetimes.

Yes, we hold family heritage within our bodies—yet we also have our spiritual lineages that may not be the same as the familial lineage you were born into. So we can remember not only our familial lineage but also our spiritual heritage.

We carry our collective remembrance in our DNA. We understand this. And here, at the holy Priestess Presence Temple, you can feel in your bones that we are one.

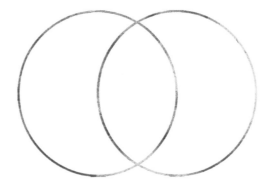

Drink, drink, drink.
Drink from the chalice.
Drink, drink, drink.
Drink from the well.
Drink, drink, drink,
Drink from the chalice.
Drink, drink, drink,
Drink from the chalice well.
Dance, sister. Dance.
Dance around the flame.
Dance around the chalice flame.
Dance around the well.
Dance around our heart.
Enter the mystery
of the galactic stars.
Enter the mystery
of our twin flame.
Enter the mystery
of who you really are.
Mem, Memnos, Mother, Matter...

Do you remember, sister? Do you remember this sacred space where the veils have dropped?

This space of great depth and beauty, where you can be who you are, fully exposed?

Do you remember being received in love, being connected to the fullness of who you are and to the fullness of others?

Do you remember being of ecstatic service to Her?

Alisa Antkowiak Adamson

THE EARTH, MY SAVING GRACE

Ah, the Earth,
my saving grace!
Touched by angels
as the wind blows o'er my face.

The sun warms me:
food of light,
bringing all that's right.

The grass a little prickly
—it wakes up my senses!
while my kitty talks to me,
so soft as she penses.

Mama Gaia, I love you!
You're all that I need:
the beautiful long grasses,
the swaying of trees.

BREATHE INTO IT LIKE LABOR ~

Life is burning away
all my fears and resistance
so that I may be reborn
—reborn to myself—
Who I really am.

The sizzle of the fire
The quivering of my womb
The smoke and the steam
The beautiful orange flame.

Burn it all away!
My ego, the small self, the limiting beliefs—
who I am not.

I am powerful,
full of light,
heart-centered,
putting down my weapons,
throwing them in the cauldron,
transmuting it all—
all for the One.

Let life move through my womb.

I feel the nervousness
I feel the pain
I feel the worry
It is not the same.

Incinerating my past,
Let it all go, to be birthed anew.

Breathe into it like labor—
I have done that enough times.
It will all be worth it,
I will come out the other side.

Mother—thank you
for bringing me home
to my witchy nature,
the magic of my bones.

The wind draws the smoke,
takes it back to her breast
to transmute into love.

Come back to nature:
Lots to burn.
So many feelings not serving.

It's time to embody what I believe,
let my light burn for all to see.

No more fear:
I AM ME.

REMEMBERING

Remembering the true meaning of the chalice
—of the blood—the life-giving blood!

I now know where it comes from.

I followed a trail in Catholicism—
the sacred rituals,
Father Bratus.

I watched his arms:
the movements, the blessings, the offerings,
the care of the sacred chalice.

Now I know where it comes from.
I remember.

It was of women,
making intentions on the power of blood
in our bodies:
anointing ourselves, then drinking.

Drinking of blood
To heal, to empower, to transmute,
to give life and creativity.
To sustain life.

The magic medicine within me,
healing this body,
unlocking the mysteries within!

The incredible beauty and power.

Now I know where it comes from.
I remember.
I remember the blood.

Ah, the power!

PREGNANT WITH MYSELF ⤳

I am pregnant with myself.
My belly is here to show it.

I need:
Rest
Recuperation
Renewal
Death
Rebirth.

The old me is dying.

The new one is growing
bigger and stronger each day,
developing more stamina.

I am she.
The she who loves.
The she with an open heart.
The one who dances, smiles, laughs, lives!

I shed the old.
I let go of the stories and attachments:
To let her be
To let her shine
To embody the greatness
To be the light and the hope
So that we may all trust in her.

Trust that she is here.
Know. Remember.
Ecstatic remembrance
of what it is to be free from the shackles.
To be truly US!
Truly me!

To know what is real—
the most amazing gift of all!

MAKING LOVE UNDER
THE FULL MOON ⤳

I am shivering with ecstasy—
The magic that I have summoned is upon me now.
The wind activates every hair on my body
The moon lights up my third eye…

My hips buck!
My womb moans!
My mouth wails!
It is alchemy of the elements.

I am alive, ignited!
I shiver, I smile…

This is why we are here now:
To tingle, to touch, to float and fly
To be wild and free!

Nothing is static—
We flow, we change, we live—
It is miraculous.

I CAN FEEL MY WINGS

I can feel my wings!
I can hear them!
They are so strong, so powerful, so colorful.

I am light,
I can hover and fly,
I am free and magical!

I vacillate from heaviness to lightness—
I know the lightness is truth.

Stay in the light to draw them up
Love them out of conflict
Love them out of resistance
Hold them, touch them, and love them up
So that we can fly together over the turbulence
to our dreams.

The rest of it is not real—
the lack, the restriction, the heaviness.
Let go and fly with me!

But we must all let go,
drop the weights
and let the wind carry us.
Feel the joy of flying in the wind
like galloping on horseback!

We are free
We are smiling
We are ecstatic!
We are light and the magic is flowing…

Anything is possible, my family,
Just believe.

RISE UP AND FLY

Drink of the mother's blood
—our moon blood—
So taboo, so edgy, so risqué!

Yet it is the greatest gift,
the true medicine, the Creatrix—direct from the womb.
What could be more magical?

Do you want to feel the ecstasy of life?
Do you want to rise up and fly
above the dullness and depression, the fog, the boredom?

Then receive Her priceless gift!
Feed and nourish yourself—
surrender, trust and fly.

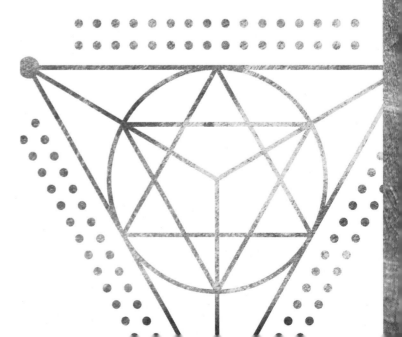

I AM A PRIESTESS ⟿

I am a priestess
I have nothing to hide.

I have magic in my hands, at my fingertips.
I can heal
I can transmute
I am here as a vessel of her love.

I am here to provide ceremony, to promote sacredness.
I am here to remember (there is so much to remember!)
and to remind others.

Mother is magic
Nature is magic
speaking to us all the time—
all the time.
Just listen, just feel, just tune in.
It is all here for us.

Be the vessel of the Goddess.
Do not hide.
Share it!
Share the amazing wealth that is the mother:
Mother Earth
Mother's love
Mother's embrace
Mother's touch.

Open up the senses
Feel the wind awaken your skin
Feel the sun on your face
Hear the wings clapping
See the bright orange flames shape shifting.

These are gifts!
Tingle and delight in them!
This is why we are here.

Be the vessel.
Be gracious for the gifts you have been given.
Allow the love to come through in every situation.

Because you are a priestess—
and that is what we do
for the ONE.

TELL THE TRUTH

Write your letters
Express your heart
Come out of hiding
Tell the truth.

Be the priestess.
There is no fear—
Only love.
Only magic.

Be the magic.
Use my tools.
This is the path of the priestess for you—
Spread your wings and fly!

SOAR! Show them who you are
so that they may also be empty vessels of love
that the light shines through—
so magnificent and bright.

Pure magic!
Let it flow!
What a gift!

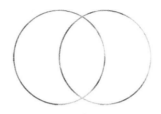

ABOUT THE AUTHOR

Alisa Antkowiak Adamson

Alisa Antkowiak Adamson (Lisie) began her journey studying Psychology at Dartmouth College while throwing the discus and hammer on the side. There she met her football playing husband, Chris, who continued on to devote his career to the sport. She worked with families in mental health and went on to get a master's in social work in hopes of making a bigger impact in the world. She counseled students in boarding schools where she and her husband lived in New Hampshire and Connecticut until she gave birth to her first child. Lisie then devoted her life to mothering, long-term breastfeeding, co-sleeping, and three more pregnancies and home births over the next fourteen years. Lisie and her family moved to California and she spent those years at home studying nutrition, health and wellness, yoga, and spirituality. Lisie has studied horse therapy and energetic healing. She is certified in Space Clearing and Reiki.
She has been married for twenty years and is the mother of Luke, 15, Grady, 12, Everet, 9, and Lenora Breeze, 5. Oklahoma is their home now—they live on a farm with dogs, cats, chickens, pigs, and horses.

Lisie is a truth-seeker and has always strayed from the mainstream. She is a lover of natural products, fresh juice, whole food, natural remedies, crystals, and essential oils. She loves nature and sunlight. She follows the moon and has studied the blood mysteries. She is now in her third year as a Priestess Initiate in the 13 Moon Mystery School lineage, where she has found meaning, magic, and sisterhood.

Lisie is expanding her gifts outside her family and into the world. Magic, mysteries, and connection to the earth and spirit is what inspires Lisie on a daily basis. She seeks to WALK AS LOVE as a way of life. Learn more at **www.Lisieatthefarm.com.**

Jeanne Adwani

~WINTER SOULSTICE~

LIGHT CALLS HER DARKNESS

Wrap me warm in your dark
tenderness,
Hold me close in the shivering
night.
Lay gentle with me in the
comfort of knowing my
return lights a way;
Hold my flame as it flickers
for you in your shadows.

Worry not how they can see
a way.
There are many ways:
The blind manage to feel it;
the scent of us is alone
a calling musk.
A deep listening will find us,
a wanting heart never forgets.

Let me surrender this day to you
Yours for the quiet time
Yours for the silent time
Yours in the cycling pattern
of this single day,
When all of me gives my light
to the chill of your night.

Wrap me warm in your dark
tenderness
Take my flame to your heart.

~HIDING~

Hiding from this aging body,
Hiding from this well-used vagina.
Hiding from the loss of allowing
another to explore me,
to desire me, to touch my wounds.

Open me wide with desire.

Hiding from the tease of love and want,
Hiding from the tender rips that
this flesh, between my legs, bleeds to
  the most delicate of swipes
  the sting of urine, the sting of soap
  the sting of water in this oozing slit

This holy portal

Hiding from desire and lust,
Hiding from sexual intimacy.
Hiding from the pain of entrance
where once this chalice, this
loving vessel gave willingly

Took in the fever of the wild

So much hiding at this Priestess's portal
of sex and vulnerability.
To feel the rise of orgasm:
To be held at the top of it
with an ancient moan

Rising to a cry of a Goddess release
So much hiding in this Crone's nest
 built of the weave of life's stories:
in the well-lived—in the betrayals,
of the loves, of the generosities;
of the trembling losses,
of the discarded imaginings
of the un-kindnesses turned to kind
of the tender heart that turns to love.
In the deep bows to gratitude.

In the Silence of Wisdom waiting

This Crone's nest, woven so tightly
of dull greys and cloudy days
of shimmering rainbows, and luminous magic
 of ecstatic wonderment, and unrequited love.
Of Creativity's fire

Burning at both ends

All the stories untold and spoken out-loud,
prison to this body's sexual yearning.
The skin of me,
thin and delicate
The Heart of me
is Love's portal:

This is where you find me now.

EVE'S WOMB ⌁

I am the chalice:
I am the cup,
I am the Holy Grail;
I am filling and pouring.

I am the womb waiting,
I am what is yet to be born.

I am death's pilgrim:
I am the Beginning
I am the End.
I am the Beginning

I am transformation's sheath:
I am She Who Serves the Athame of Love:
   I cut to the chase.
   I clear the way.
   I wait at the Gate.
I am the wind in your wings,
I am a storm that erodes:
I am the turbulence of a million breaths;
I am the breath of you.

I am Gaia:
I am a blue marble floating in space,
I am the ancient maple
I am every root weaving
I am the ley of the land
I am the crown of the mountain.
I am the forest path:
I am Persphone's seed.

I am bone and sinew:
I am the soul of your feet;
I am Adam's rib
I am Satan's apple
I am Eve's womb.

SIDARTHA'S JOURNEY ～

I am the mystery.

Will I find myself?
I took them all…

A Path. A road.
A journey.
A maze. A labyrinth.
A spiral.

I walked. I flew.
I danced.
I sat. I dreamt.
I pondered.

I smoked. I drank.
I sniffed.
I fucked. I loved.
I left.

I am a mystery.

My quest has calloused my feet.
Armored my heart.
Stained my skin
in techno color:
a living banner
of life's possibilities.

I am a mystery.

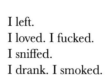

I left.
I loved. I fucked.
I sniffed.
I drank. I smoked.

I pondered.
I dreamt. I sat.
I danced.
I flew. I walked.

A spiral.
A labyrinth. A maze.
A journey.
A road. A path.

I took them all back to myself.

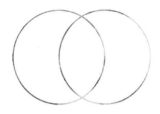

ABOUT THE AUTHOR

Jeanne Adwani

Jeanne Adwani is an artist/creatrix, a Muse, a poet, a Creativity Coach, a Light and energy shifter, a Sister on the path of the 13 Moon Mystery School. She is a hair 'healer' and owner of "Be Hair Now" salon. Jeanne is the co-creator of the beautiful experience of Evenstar's Chalice in downtown Ypsilanti, MI. She is an Anointing Priestess; creating a line of essential blends called Sovereign Elements.

Jeanne hold the space on this Earth life for paradox; that standing between the worlds of duality where Love and fear share the same space, at the same time, and need the same balance.

Her roots are deep in Earth-based Spirituality, honoring the Divine Feminine as we rise again to nurture, celebrate, and empower All life with Love and wisdom.

Jeanne listens to and plays with the magic of the elements that are around and within us all: Earth, Fire, Air, Water, and Spirit tell our stories, and connect us to the sacredness of all life.

She accesses the energy and 'stories' of tarot, numerology, astrology, and the deep listening to Spirit and silence to find a path to an understanding of personal wisdom and self-empowerment.

Jeanne's 'Heart's desire' is to practice the Path of Love, peace and kindness, in the "Be Here Now," to laugh as much as possible, and 'To turn to love no matter what'. Namaste'.

Visit her poetry blog at **www.geezergirl.org.**

Julie Anderson

MY WAY THROUGH ↝

I am a wobbly priestess in earthen form.
Stuckness is my tool of transformation.

There's only one way through that allows me to move.
There's only one way through each moment to get to the other side.

The earth moves through me easily. Steadily like lava, like water, like dirt, like air.
It's all the same.
My perception is different; all is the same.

Stuckness is my way of being. There's only perception that lives in that mind.
I allow the flow to flow. In my mind, I open to allow that as well.

All rivers of emotions, stuck there for eternities, are gone in a blink of an eye.
In the blink of an eye, all stuckness remains.

I'm noticed and unnoticed.
I'm noticed as the observer; I am unnoticed as someone not worthy.
All is in the perception of the observer and the observed.

There's lessons to be remembered;
And there is nothing forgotten.

When a piece of my stuckness gets in the way
of me, there's a blessing.

Judgment, and self-righteousness: it all matters.
Judgment, and self-righteousness: it does not exist.
There's always choice in those moments.

When in flow, the choice disappears: there's simply allowing, understanding;
not understanding and allowing.
The self-made priestesses know this.
The ego priestess does not.

As an ego priestess I cannot exist only in my mind.
Let go of all that is in the way; the mind included.

In the way, is the way.
Let go and allow the flow.
The pulsating movement of the earth is the way.

Follow the energy to your enlightenment, I say.
Follow the energy to the next step and the next; the energy knows.

The priestess true and on the path follows easily in the emptiness of her chalice.
Fill yourself up with the void of nothing.
I try to listen and hear myself.
Nothing exists; nothing is predetermined.

That age-old feeling is simply a way through.
That mirror from a loved one in pain is the way through.
The way through is the path.

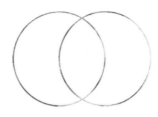

ABOUT THE AUTHOR

Julie Anderson

Julie Anderson is a Priestess on hiatus, currently inhabiting an Art Students life. Insta: @juliemichelleanderson

Jane Astara Ashley

LET ME HOLD YOU ⁓

Surrender to my flow

Let me hold you,
Sweet Loving daughter

You are not alone

Let me be present
in space
through the heat
of your love

Rise to the unfurling
of your inner rose
to meet ALL

Out of this grows everything you could ever desire
or feel connected to in this lifetime

You are here now

Grounded...
Delivering the SEED from the void,
Anointing it with LOVE

Open to receive me
for I am Presence.

I AM your Mother
I AM your sister
I AM your daughter

We have never been apart

Beloved,

All the threads weave together,

to reveal the tapestry
of the ONE heart

You were born for this...

Fully open now the sweet beauty of your crowned heart
to all those who gather to witness

Bloom together,
for this is the way forward, my love...

Let me hold you

Turn towards me
Turn within

I AM here now.

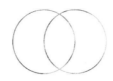

ABOUT THE AUTHOR

Jane Astara Ashley

Jane Astara Ashley, CEO and Publisher of Flower of Life Press, Transpersonal Psychotherapist, Modern Day Priestess, Ceremonial Guide

First and foremost, Astara is a Publisher: words and books the catalysts fueling her journey, and enlightening the expansive tribe of "Evolutionaries" who are searching for a better life for themselves and their families. Flower of Life Press began with a conversation, and a challenge: how can we create an author-focused company that is dynamic and entrepreneurial, a true home for the "voices of transformation" we are committed to? Astara has walked this road for more than ten years, and Flower of Life Press has mirrored her path through the maze of life's challenges. Along the way, she has gathered a group of authors around the sacred fire of truth and shepherded their wise words into books, brands, speeches, and powerful marketing platforms. Astara is the founder of the best-selling New Feminine Evolutionary book series, which consists of six collaborative books and hundreds of authors. Through these potent and Divinely Feminine writing collaborations, Astara holds a sacred container for women to claim their power and their voice. She is the publisher and designer of the book you now hold in your hands.

Books are just one facet of Astara's true passion—to help women elevate their consciousness, lives, and businesses by distilling their essence and creating resonance and connec-

tion through their messages. Since truly authentic writing requires a deepened resonance, the job of Publisher has been redefined by Astara's own expansion into becoming a multi-dimensional Divine Feminine Leader, and a 5th year 13-Moon Mystery school Priestess Initiate. It is this immersion in energy dynamics and spirituality that distinguishes her work and elevates her author's experiences beyond a traditional publishing relationship.

In order to better serve her Global clientele of authors and entrepreneurs, Astara has just unveiled her Signature writing course "Sisters of Light Divine Writing Journey"—full of the inspiration and instruction that has helped so many writers overcome blocks, uncover truths, and step forward into the global conversation.

FREE video training with workbook:
"Bestseller Priestess: 3 sacred steps to becoming a best-selling author who prospers from her potent work" available at
www.bestsellerpriestess.com/bestseller-priestess

FREE online private Writer's Group:
www.facebook.com/groups/publishedpriestess

Brooke Bowman

SANCTUARY

She knocks.
Open your doors.
Something is burning;
It's hot … and only getting hotter.

There's no more space inside:
Fear is no longer an excuse.

We are all scared.
There is no other way out.

Open your doors!
The waters are coming!

Feel Her power;
Let Her flow in...
Open, open, open.

The flames go out.

Within the darkness, the light is bright:
Warm and welcoming;

You are home.

Left: Art by Brooke Bowman

RETURN OF THE SUN ୶

The solar logos illuminates.
Divine light glistens on Her waters.

A chalice arises on the surface;
She holds all of it:
everything that has ever been felt
seeping back into Her.

Emptiness is re-born.
Into the darkness, She beckons.

You are safe in here;
in the void, there is nothing to fear.

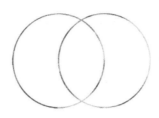

ABOUT THE AUTHOR

Brooke Bowman

Brooke is a student of the magic and the mystery. She teaches transformation through the practices of yoga, meditation, qi gong and reiki. She is currently training to be a death doula and working with the elderly population providing support and healing in the end stages of life. She is a traveler, nature lover, foodie, and ecstatic dancer. She lives in Boston with her two children.

Rebecca Cavender

PRIMORDIAL MOTHER

Enter me,
the Cosmic Womb of Love,
the Primordial Mother of All.
I am the Universal Shakti,
the Everlasting Light of Life.

Feed from me.
I offer you the
honey-crystals of
sweet surrender.

I give you your
life to suckle from me.
I am yours to take:
the embodiment of your greatest desires
your most sacred purpose.

From my belly,
I gift you
your gifts,
your holy knowing,
your sweet remembrance.

All I want,
my love,
is you.

All I crave,
my love,
is your flourishing flame of light
brightly burning
for all you Love,
for all you align with,
for all that brings you ecstatic joy.

This life,
This eternal life
is yours to taste.

(I give you sweet cakes;
please lick the sugar from your lips.)

Will you surrender to the
Love that awaits you?

This Mystery is
your
mystery.
This depth,
this lesson,
is the return to
your
Essence,
your
Fire,
your
unique Sound of Light.

I come to you,
lay roses at your feet,
anoint your vessel with the
Wine of All Gods
and
welcome
you
Home.

UNION ~

I anoint your graceful union,
Your starlight wisdom,
the truth of sacred home.

Lay your head across my vast sky,
as I penetrate your depth of heart.

You are the Beloved of My Beloved:
My Beloved, Your Beloved,
One.

DEVOTION ~

I feel the warmth of your flame
the heat of your dance
the way your tongue flicks in erotic union.

You are the flame of my heart,
the one who sings my soul,
burning me to ecstasy.

I am the dance of your heart
The flame of your soul
The flickering light of ecstatic union.

Enter me.
Feel my heat.
Walk through the gate of my devotion.

ECSTATIC POETRY OF LIFE⤳

I touch the soft light,
bright in essence,
until my fingers slip
into grace
a hush across a field,
a reminder of
another season,
another place
     -     The door to which ajar -
peeking in, I
glimpse
a reflection
of who I once was
when land was gold,
when ocean
kissed lakes,
when Love
was All,
when the heartbeat
of humanity
worshiped its divinity.

What succulence,
honey-tipped tongue
of radiance
That time,
That woman,
knew
to embrace the
ecstatic poetry of Life.

QUEEN OF DEATH ‿

Don't be afraid
    It's only a little death:
            death of the moment
            death of seed
            death of birth

I only want now.

Will you plunge into me—into my liquid depths?

I hold the darkness for you
            where stars collide in union so sweet
            the scent of release—
            It feels like home

I am your altar.
Decorate me with your silent awe—the way you gasp for more
            lips to fingers
            fingers to taste
            taste of the sea
            (the sea you crossed to cum to me)

Give me your aches—your fears
            I'll bless them with my mouth
            and
            you'll take back the night.

PRIMAL GODDESS ~

I am the fire of life:
Your yoni portal,
your everlasting light
—the orgasmic birth of your holy presence.

I lick up your spine in remembrance of your ecstatic flame.

I lick up your spine:
—a lover of infinite proportions.

I lick up your spine:
—in love with
your body essence,
your scent,
your musk

      ...the way I swallow you.
      ...the way I swallow you.

You are here to be swallowed whole.

Let me taste you, your erotic fire.

Ohhhh … you taste like dew-light,
like charcoal and mud,
like the sweet honeysuckle that weeps at night.

Ahhhh…
I take you in.
I take you into my pleasure body.
I unfold for you.
Unfold, unfold, unfold.

My yoni fire-light-heat:
That juice,
that life,
that love.

I pierce you with my penetrative touch,
Then suck you,
like manna:
a feast for gods,
for the earth,
for the cosmos,
            thrusting light to orgasmic creative bliss.

This is your creation.
This is how you create.
This is how you move.
This is how you connect to the

straight line between god and fire and man.

Make love to the earth,
to the starry earth,
the drumming fire of life.

Drum drum drum drum
Drum.

Drum drum drum drum
Drum.

Drum drum drum drum
Drum.

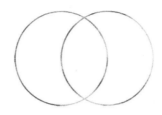

ABOUT THE AUTHOR

Rebecca Cavender

Rebecca Cavender is the Priestess Presence Temple's scribe and oracle. She has mentored with Elayne Kalila, Diana DuBrow, Ariel Spilsbury, and Eden Amadora.

She is a professional, intuitive writer—and proudly autistic—living in Yakima Washington … a beautiful desert valley in Washington State upon the traditional land of the Yakama people.

This is where she calls home after living in five countries on four continents—including Myanmar. She's an international best-selling author of a guidebook for expats and co-authored the temple's #1 selling book, *The Sacred Call of the Ancient Priestess*, with Elayne Kalila Doughty.

But what really matters to her is activating and honoring our sacred self-expression so we feel whole. This takes listening to our authentic voice and knowing that even (especially!) if it's a divergent, different voice, it matters … in fact, it can help change the world.

Rebecca's priestessing comes through her Nordic ancestors and spiritual lineages that include the medicine of writing, sound, touch, anointing, ritual, and shamanic journeys. From this inspired place of love, Rebecca intuitively scribes words in a uniquely catalyzing and lyrical voice, offering them as medicine so you know you belong.

Rebecca provides the following services to help you access your sacred self-expression:
- Writing circles
- Bespoke coaching & accountability for your writing projects
- 1:1 sessions—to have a direct experience of your creative, fiery, True Self
- Intuitive copywriting and editing

…discover more at **www.rebeccacavender.com** and check out her best-selling poetic anthology, *Sacred Reunion: Love Poems to the Masculine & Feminine* on Amazon.

Dianne Chalifour

OH, SACRED MASCULINE

Oh, Sacred Masculine:
It does not interest me, who you think you are
beneath the stories, the ones you speak, inflating your skin.

I see your truth: I see your fears; I see your essence.

You've lost your way. Forgotten yourself.
Take off your masks; it's time to unveil.
There's no more time to waste.

You want to be naked, passion in the flesh
yet you know not what it means to truly strip free,
to stand before another and truly be seen,
beneath it all:
unwavering surrender, breathless and free.

Oh, yes:
Trembling remembrance
of most precious truth.
Climb out of the ashes and burn with me,
for there is no fire like the one inside

Stand up, rise with me,
surrender your mask.
Then and only then, shall we truly be free!

I SEE YOU

Death in the mirror, the fallow reflection:
Who art thou? My eyes cannot see.
Why is it you come, day in and day out,
seeking life, the blood red?

Wait...
I see you; I hear a tender cry:
the familiar, the merciful weep.
It is you, and yes, I do know.

ROSA MYSTICA

Oh sister, my sister.
Come, let me dust off this debris:
the dirt, the insults, the sorrow and shame.

Come to the circle, we bathe you anew.

Breathe in my sweet love.
Rosa mystica.
Inhale as gently, the anointed one, you lay.
Breathe in my sweet love.

The circle we weave, will never be broken.
It's alchemical gold, fine silvery thread,
dancing through time,
on dragons we ride!

DANCE OF LIFE

In this dance of life, I flow
through streams of conscious connection
into unseen realms of desire, passion,
of ecstasy with the beloved.

Divine nuances kiss my feet and trickle up my limbs,
wrapping around my womb, continuing up my breasts
divine sustenance, nourishing my heart
meeting my voice
then flowing like honey off my tongue:
dripping like magical, golden sunshine.

The beloved finding expression through my being,
and I, the vessel in which love flows.
My third eye kisses the earth,
to Her I bow, in sweet devotion,
surrendering to Her in ways only She can guide:
Here, I surrender to Love's ecstatic embrace.
We are One.

LOVE'S SWIRLING SURRENDER ∾

Salt water sprays, up over the rocks, crash
into new form, rolling beneath
spiraling back to the surface...
drawing one in, then emerging into light,
feeling the call of sweet surrender.

Always the chance to wash away and renew.
How does one walk past and not see?
Not feel the drawing in the depths of soul?

How I long to show you, to take you there
on the wings of love's embrace.

Beneath the shadows, there's nothing to fear:
nothing to hold onto, for nothing is real.
Surrender with me, I shall take you there.

We'll soar through the air,
dive into Her waters, and swirl with Her spirals:
intoxicating and free.
We let Her have Her way with us,
ecstatic breathlessness,
penetrating delight, crash-through sweet surrender.
We merge,
re-emerge,
into the light—something so new, so sweet—
through love's embrace,
together we feel,
only Love is real.

PRIESTESS ⤸

I AM a Priestess.
My motivations do not lie in the earthly concerns that visit me in the pass between the worlds.

For I walk in the mists where whispers lead my heart.
This path is not one of ease, though surely one of grace.
This realm of the physical calls me here and to, demands the logical.
Yet,

I AM a Priestess.
My motivations do not lie in the earthly concerns that visit me in the pass between the worlds.

This heart is the tuner that receives the signals
of pain and sorrow in the eyes of the people.
The warrior in my womb: oh, she steps to the front
where no woman or no man shall fall by the side.

I AM a Priestess.
My motivations do not lie in the earthly concerns that visit me in the pass between the worlds.

My sword is my truth that shall cut through the lies of the ego.
With eyes to see and ears to hear, I stand upon the threshold
and hold the key for your soul:
Liberation is not won less you pass through this gate.

I AM a Priestess.
My motivations do not lie in the earthly concerns that visit me in the pass between the worlds.

My presence is a whisper, you may wonder what nudges you so.
This power within, you may not know of, nor patriarch nor force:
Igniting soul fires wherever she goes,
dropping the fire within your already broken heart:
explosion into chaos, alchemical feast of frenzy,
only to land onto new ground upon Her earth.

For I AM a Priestess,
Whose awakening has arrived upon this altar of destiny.

Come, taste the sweetness in the mists between the worlds
where I wait to hear your call.

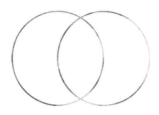

ABOUT THE AUTHOR

Dianne Chalifour

Dianne Chalifour is a passionate, transformational guide within the healing arts. She is the owner of a wellness center in the New Hampshire seacoast born through her passionate calling to offer tools and services to assist in the awakening, connection and shifting of our human evolutionary process of living a soul inspired life.

In addition to in person and remote 1:1 energy healing sessions, Dianne offers in person anointing sessions. She also guides in person temple sister circles to allow women to come together in a safe space for inner work and re-connection with their feminine body wisdom.

Dianne serves as a type of midwife for her clients to reach deep into their own inner knowing and step forward empowered into the life that is waiting for them. Through her own journey on her continually evolving spiritual path, Dianne is committed to the path of Priestessing; to serving from her heart where her path leads her and being in service to the greater shift under way!

Dianne is co-author of the best-selling books, *Sacred Body Wisdom Igniting The Flame of Our Divine Humanity*, and *Sacred Reunion: Love Poems to the Masculine & Feminine—An Anthology* both published by Flower of Life Press. Contact Dianne at **www.earthharmonywellness.com.**

Aurora Farber

TANGO FOR ONE

I feel your rhythm
In the heart of me,
Longing for something greater,
Something deep, mystical and undivided.

I yearn for this connection,
For you to guide and lead me
In a dance
That sets me free.

Trusting each cue
I follow in fluidity.
Each step becoming more and more myself
Our sacred union, danced in the mystery.

It took years
To find you,
My dance card filled with
Endless, empty rotations.

Not until I looked within
Did I find your eyes staring back at me,
My own inner masculine waiting for the day
I stepped forward and asked to dance.

Instead I held you away
Or projected you onto others,
Hoping to be saved
Or completed with fragments of another.

Sometimes I caught glimpses of you in dreams
Disguised as hero, pop star, dwarf,
Shaping you into something I revered
Or something undesired.

Withered and torn,
I finally tossed my dance card away,
No longer willing to politely wait
And be chosen.

Instead I paused and listened
And then, *I chose myself.*
In sovereign alignment, you emerged from within,
Whispering words of our greatness.

In that first step, my heart raced
Your powerful frame holding me,
Igniting my feminine fire
As we danced in freedom, joy and ecstasy.

Now and forevermore,
I choose to follow
The rhythm of our
Our united hearts.

I long for movement
And wait for stillness.
I embrace passion
And hunger for the pause of anticipation.

With you in me, I am in balance,
Dying, living, being reborn
In every step of this sacred
Tango for one.

~ECSTASY~

Ecstatic bliss
Shakti fire
Free
Wild
Powerful
Filled with desire

Making love to my soul
I undulate
Riding these waves of pleasure
Simply for pleasure's sake

Magenta, orange, hot pink
Velvet honey
Drips
Ignites…

I open myself more and more and more
To this ecstatic delight

Who am I to deny myself of this?
This freedom to be completely open,
Undenied
In complete love and devotion
To my sweet liberation

Who am I to shy away
From sharing my shakti fire with others?

Because I fear ridicule,
Judgment,
Shame
Or separation?

How can I deny the world this gift,
This pleasure,
This union of body, heart and soul?

Holy body, I call on thee
To imprint this deliciousness
And make me crave more

Let it ROAR from my yoni
Like a siren's song of temptation and desire!

I devour this now
And pray for the hunger pains
To remind me
That this is not frivolous, vain, or selfish

This is essential, life-altering,
Soul-stirring medicine
That feeds me…
That feeds us all.

Remind me sacred vessel
Because I'm afraid I will forget
Yet again
As busyness consumes me
And I put my ecstasy casually aside.

Already I hear the drums of necessity calling…

So how do I remember this feeling?
How dare I forget!

I sit in silence and ask for a reminder…

And then SHE says,

Honey, I am always here for you
This flame NEVER goes out

Just call me
Your hips know
My number by heart

I am here, baby
Waiting for you
To come play
In ecstasy.

～WISE WOMAN～

Wise Woman
Where are you?
All my life I've searched for you.
Wanting to know you,
Longing to be you.

Seeking, searching, studying
Traveling, voyaging,
Lost in an endless quest
To find you.

I *need* you and your wisdom because I wonder,
Will I ever know anything for sure?
Will I ever be wise enough?

And where do I find you?
I've searched far and wide
In books, on mountain tops
In the darkest shadows
Looking for the gold.

And still it's not enough…
You are nowhere to be found.

I caught a glimpse of you once,
In the eyes of a woman in a magazine.
Those sly eyes daring me to paint you.
With each stroke I fleshed you out
To remind me of who might become.

But just yesterday you came to me
In the shower of all places,
An unexpected memory of my teenage self.

My excitement, at 13,
When I bought my first outfit
On layaway.
Each week, my allowance saved
For these clothes
Chosen as an expression of *my* style.

Dark, rich, velvet black culottes
A white high-necked, ruffled blouse
With shiny black buttons.

Ah-ha! Your favorite colors.
Black and white
The colors of simplicity.

I see myself now at 13
In my mind's eye
Wearing my first choice of adornment
To step into the world as *me.*

Wise Woman,
I'm just realizing now,
Finally, at age 50…
There was nowhere to go to look for you.

You were never outside me,
But always within,
Waiting for me to claim you and
Wear you proudly in the world.

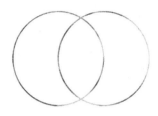

ABOUT THE AUTHOR

Aurora Farber

Aurora Anurca Farber, Feminine Leadership Coach, Intuitive Guide, Priestess Presence Temple Guide Trainer, 13 Moon Mystery School Trained Priestess, Writer, & Speaker is on a mission to help women ignite their "Feminine Fire" the 3 flames of POWER, LOVE and WISDOM that are the key to awakening the new feminine evolutionary consciousness that will heal our world. She helps women burn away limiting beliefs, align with their feminine moon rhythm, and embody their mythic purpose in the world.

Aurora holds honors degrees in Literature and Foreign Language, along with a professional certification in Coaching. She is a Priestess Initiate of The 13 Moon Mystery School and has been on the path since 2012. As a Temple Guide Mentor of the Priestess Presence Temple, she mentors women in how to create sacred space and become Temple Guides in their communities. She is a co-author of three books in the The New Feminine Evolutionary series: The New Feminine Evolutionary; Pioneering the Path to Prosperity; and Sacred Body Wisdom.

Through private coaching, online programs, women circles and retreats, Aurora creates sacred spaces for women to be held, witnessed, and loved exactly as they are right here, right now. Her guiding vision is a world of women claiming their creative powers, loving their body temples, and being beacons of fierce wisdom as they burn away archaic, limiting beliefs and light the world on fire with love.

Discover more at **www.aurorafarber.com.**

Catherine J. Franchetti

~THE SEED~

We shrink from our power
hide it from the world
and do our best to hide it from ourselves.

We see this power as inconvenient:
    What are we to do with it, after all
    brandishing it doesn't suit us,
    doesn't feel right.

Holding it within, we must pay a price
      and the price is too dear:
    Alienation from ourselves;
Yet we fear those who don't accept
don't understand
feel threatened by it
      Not our place
      Not our right
      Not our strength
      Not our sight.

It belongs to someone else;
    Someone with more capacity
    more courage
    more insight
    more supports
    more advantages
    more anything...
...Not us.

Yet you, dear one, hold power in your heart
and infinite possibility in your hand

to wield gently—and with love—
walking the path of the heart
guided by the knowing that lies within you.

Yes, it is there
No matter how soundly you have buried it

Like a seed awaiting its time
    to sprout
    to bloom
    to become what is meant.

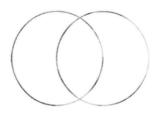

ABOUT THE AUTHOR

Catherine J. Franchetti

Catherine is an advanced energy practitioner, certified Warrior Goddess Facilitator, herbalist − and a certified accountant. She supports women to increase their energy and reclaim their essence. She dreams of a world where women are living into the fullest version of themselves. Too many women are missing out on their own lives, and too many moms miss out on their kids' lives as well. This world needs us at our best, because as each woman gains strength, so do her children, so do her friends, and so does her community.

When she's not spending time with her husband, sons, and granddaughter, or out in the forest around her home in Canada, you can find Catherine happily immersed in learning something new and fascinating.

It's time to live an amazing, energetic, joyful life.

Find out more at **www.NaturalHealingConnection.com.**

Ari Haff

I REMEMBER

I remember…
water, fire
stone and ash;
faces, symbols
joyful dance.

I remember…
opening, emptying
flowing
sacred oils, temples
knowing.

I remember…
shadow dives
boundless flight;
honeyed hives
the sight.

I remember…
sisterhood, circles
and grace
distant, yet not
through time and space…

I remember…
I remember…

I Remember.

Left: Art by Ari Haff

Art by Ari Haff

Left & right pages: Art by Ari Haff

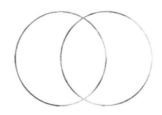

ABOUT THE AUTHOR

Ari Haff

As Gatekeeper of The Sapphire Temple, **Ari Haff** is deeply committed to holding temple space for all ages and genders guided by the study of Divine Archetypes, the wisdom of the Sisterhood of the Rose, and the teachings of the 13 Moon Mystery School, derived from The 13 Moon Oracle by Ariel Spilsbury.

Through The Sapphire Temple, Ari offers monthly moon circles, guided divine archetypal study, as well as personal and group ceremonies. Ari also conducts varied events designed as sacred deepening experiences into essential oils, botanicals, sound, art, oracle, and embodiment practices.

Ari is a practicing Scent Priestess of the Emerald Temple. She is devoted to the sacred art of Anointing and to sharing the powerful gift of sacred oils. She continues her journey of remembrance as a Mentor and Temple Pillar in the Priestess Presence Temple where she found her path as a Priestess along with the beauty of true synergy and sisterhood.

As a Virtual World Creatrix and Artist, Ari builds beautiful realistic meeting spaces, temples, and sacred art in the virtual world. These spaces are designed to bridge the physical distance of global communities, spark remembrance, and offer a joyful reflection of the nature of our user created reality.

Ari is Mom to six wonderful children. She lives in rural Michigan with her family and their menagerie of cuddly cats, adorable goldendoodle puppies and one seemingly invincible goldfish.

You can connect with Ari at **www.TheSapphireTemple.com**
Instagram: arihaff; thesapphiretemple
FB: Ari Haff @sapphirepriestess; The Sapphire Temple

Taida Horozovic

~I SEE YOU, SISTER~

I see you, sister

I feel the buds of your genius bursting
—it seems sudden but it's not—
You've had this song in you the whole time

I love you, Sister,
and I thank you:
you make me better
through this communication,
this song.

Holding this vibration
is a gift
I am honored
to hold it with you:
To Grow This Love Together.

You are love
You are needed
You are not alone
You are important
You do not need fixing
I am not here to fix you
You are not here to fix me
We've always known this truth

We sing our song free and loud
The fire warms us
Our skin wears the scent of flowers

Our curiosity to be on the path of love
ignites the fire
and uncovers more ways
to serve love

Together we dance across the skies

You are fierce,
powerful, free

Your generous heart
knows no bounds.
Sister Love
you belong

We are united
from within.
Ever evolving, our
hearts growing together

Soar, Woman!
You are love!
Goddess holds you!
You are Her!

I sing this song from my heart

Love is the compass of our hearts
It's how we can always find our way.

I am humbled to be here with you.

Left photo: "Embrace of the Tree is Eternal" by Taida Horozovic

I DON'T NEED TO KNOW
YOU TO LOVE YOU ∼

it is my ancient magic
packed in a smile:
open to new
waves
skies

I see myself clothed in love:
it is divine!
a goddess sitting simple

in all her shine.

WHATEVER MY HEART DESIRES ∼

The wind whistles and sings
Fallen leaves dance and twirl in the air

I know this ancient song
It is whirling through my hair

My body knows this dance
My body loves this dance

I'm gonna treat myself
To whatever my heart desires
—right now!

I am abundance even when I seem bare—
My nakedness attests to it.

*Right photo: "Walking Between the Worlds
with Trees" by Taida Horozovic*

"Energy is Love" by Taida Horozovic

"Deep in the Colors of Your Love" by Taida Horozovic

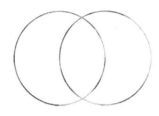

ABOUT THE AUTHOR

Taida Horozovic

Taida Horozovic is on her Priestess Path to Walk As Love. A communications professional for over twenty years, Taida loves helping organizations thrive.

As a nomadic soul, she is happiest when she's outdoors, near trees and taking pictures in nature. Most recently, her inspiration is writing poetry, mandala-making with flowers, and deepening into which crystals resonate with her light-and-shadow-qualities-work.

She is a plant-based diet enthusiast and loves to travel.

Connect with Taida at **taida.horozovic@gmail.com** and instagram @tainomadica.

Photo right: "Soul Song in the Body of Water" by Taida Horozovic

Elizabeth Locey

DROPPING THE VEILS ⌒

I am verdant field, alive with sunshine and
wind rippling through.

I am fragrant pine forest, my perfume intoxicating all
who encounter me.

I am bird on branch, cocking my head to bring piercing clarity.

I am aurora, gilding edges of clouds and leaf-tips with my
ephemeral, perennial love.

I am ocean wave, tumbling grains of beach sand with
my foamy caress.

I am night sound: chirp of cricket and cicada, hoot of owl,
breath of wind rolling fallen leaves through grass.

I am beauty. I am understanding. I am eternal.

I am.

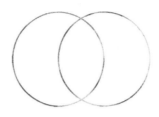

ABOUT THE AUTHOR

Elizabeth Locey

Elizabeth Locey, Ph.D, is a priestess-trained teacher, author and channel who speaks richly to spiritual entrepreneurs who are called to serve the world at a higher level, yet cannot see how to make the leap.

Elizabeth helps dissolve blocks around resources (time, money, know-how), and the seemingly impregnable ramparts of worthiness and will-I-lose-everything-if-I-am-truly-seen? A long-term client says of her: "Elizabeth shines when guiding people through their darkest fears into Love."

Until 2010, Elizabeth was an award-winning professor & scholar of French literature and Women's Studies. She abruptly traded in her purple pen for a crystal-topped staff in order to midwife more magick and healing into the world through Akashic Records, crystals, alchemical transmutation, and bringing the interdimensional Mythic Self into form in the 3D world. If you've been feeling like an outsider and are apologizing (undercharging) for your sacred gifts, and would like to own them proudly and offer them to the world without getting in your own way, reach out to Elizabeth for a conversation about awakening your Legendary Self. In addition to her private Oracle work, Elizabeth teaches classes on intuition, crystals, and Mythic Allies such as Dragons, Unicorns, Faeries, and more.

Elizabeth is a contributing author to a number of best-sellers, including *The Power of Being a Woman.* Find her author portal on amazon.com.

Follow her and download her many free transmissions at **www.elizabethlocey.com.**

Christine Machiraju

STANDING AT THE EDGE OF A CLIFF

Standing at the edge of a cliff, toes dangling, ready to jump
my gaze focused on the bottom in the distance
But you touch me with your breath,
you caress me with your lips and guide my gaze upward.

I am stunned by the glory of your crimson smile
blush of pink, depth of purple.

You remind me that you are always with me:
Always
and forever
You remind me that I am always with you.

Your sunrise smile reminds me everyday that
there is no struggle,
there is no suffering.

This is all just a play:
the earth is our stage
we are all actors.

You are the director, producer and audience.
You flow through each of us
playing with love, hate, and bliss while remaining still.

Each morning, you remind me that there is endless beauty:
rippling, rippling, rippling beauty
flowing out your every pore.

You grace us with your tender touch
your brilliant smile
your endless kisses.

You remind us that we are always in your womb,
 in your heart,
in your loving gaze.

I drop off the cliff of my suffering
into your loving arms.

I remember:
My love, I have never left you;
you have never left me.
We are one.

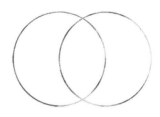

ABOUT THE AUTHOR

Christine Machiraju

Christine Machiraju Christine was born legally blind. The vision she lacked in the physical world enabled her to see multi-dimensionally. As a small child, she was able to see angels and communicate with the deceased. She was also able to sense illness in people.

At the age of 21 she traveled to India to work in an orphanage aShe furthered her study of yoga, ayurveda, meditation and Indian Classical dance. Her connection with Spirit gave her a sense of deep peace that she wanted to share with others.

She returned to cdCanada and opened her own yoga and healing centre. She brought yoga to the little city where she lived and her community programs are still running twenty years later.

Christine has done one on one sessions for the past 20 years. She's used the Vedic sciences of palmistry, yoga, ayurveda and chanting to help people recover from addiction, empower people with mental health issues find balance, overcome infertility and so much more.

Christine is now helping women step into their own confidence and assisting men in opening their hearts. She is passionate about helping people love themselves and find their own personal connection with Spirit through ritual, chanting, yoga, meditation and sacred travel. Contact Christine at **www.livinginharmony.ca.**

Quadira McLeod

I SEE YOU ﹏

I know who you are
Looking deep into your eyes
I feel your pain   your suffering
Your deep   unbearable sorrow

Come   sit beside me
And tell me all of your troubles
I will listen with an
Open heart

I will wrap you in a blanket of Love
With Ease for your pillow
I will sing you sweet songs
Of Healing and Possibility

I will bring you a bowl
Of nourishing Hugs
And a warm cup of Tenderness
I will wipe away your tears
With soft Compassion

I will hold you until
Your breathing is calm
And you see your inner Strength
When you look into my eyes

I will hold you
Until you feel the fear subside
Until Grace and Hope
Fill the emptiness inside

Now breathe in Love
Exhaling anger and pain
Breathe in Joy
Exhaling tension and sorrow

Breathe in Peace
Feel yourself held
In the arms of the Beloved
You are free to Love once more

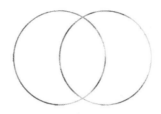

ABOUT THE AUTHOR

Quadira McLeod

Quadira McLeod is a graduate of Indiana University (Bloomington, IN) with a BA in Anthropology and English Literature. She has over 20 years of experience as a writer and editor, and worked at Watson-Guptill Publications, where she was editorial assistant, and Clarion Books, where she was the assistant to the director of promotion and publicity. Quadira has extensive freelance writing and editing experience, and is the youngest daughter of children's author Nancy D. Watson and illustrator Aldren A. Watson, and the sister of children's author Clyde Watson and illustrator Wendy Watson.

Quadira owned her own business for many years, Golden Touch Designs Writing & Editing. She is a former member of the NMBA (New Mexico Book Association). She is the author of the children's books *Down in the Valley, Nothing to Do,* and *Chloe the Bear* series as well as *Lavender & Lace: Recipes from My Victorian Tea Room* (all awaiting publication). Her potery is published in the college literary magazine, "The Dancing Star". Quadira has also studied with poets Nancy D. Watson, Alan Dugan, and Laurel Blossom. She can be reached at **quadirasophia@gmail.com.**

Abigail Mensah-Bonsu

~I AM GODDESS~

I am Goddess.
Goddess I am.

I am awake,
opening my eyes to the wonders
of the universe as Me.
I am Goddess.

Mysteries unfolding:
Priestess, Medicine Woman:
I am Goddess.

My tongue translating the golden
frequency of the Divine:
Prophetess, I am.
I am Goddess.

I roll with my Divine Posse of angels, archangels,
guides and guardians, the Wise Ones,
the Masters of Light:
I am Goddess.

I Illuminate in the deep,
ancient wisdom of my inner knowing.
I honor myself, my work, my life, my gifts:
I am Goddess.

I am a queen, woman,
wife, mother.
I am Goddess.

I am divine. I am love.
I am fire. I am passion.
I am Goddess.

I am worthy. I am rebirth.
I am joy;
I am Goddess.

I dig my roots into the sacred earth and
drink deep from the well of healing,
nourishment and passion.
I am Goddess.

I live an empowered life,
aligned with my soul expression
and higher consciousness
I am Goddess.

I co-create with divinity.
I am divinity unfolding.
I am Goddess.

I am fierce like the black jaguar,
bold like the lioness.
I am Goddess.

I roll with the dragons
and the phoenix,
a conduit for divine love.
I am Goddess.

My energy, expansive:
Magnetized to the divine frequency of abundance,
prosperity, beauty, wisdom, grace and power.
I am Goddess.

I come home to my Divine Essence;
I transform the lives and
ignite the sacred fires within those who step
into my presence.
I Am Goddess

I anchor Heavenly powers in the creation
of my life and my reality.
I thrive, unleash.
And rise.
I am Goddess
Goddess I am.

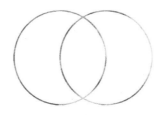

ABOUT THE AUTHOR

Abigail Mensah-Bonsu

Abigail Mensah-Bonsu is an Intuitive Quantum Goddess Coach, a Leader, a Divine Feminine Activator and a Multidimensional Healer.

She is a Catalyst for Expansion pioneering the birth of "New Ways of Being" into this realm. She lovingly serves to remind you of what you really are beyond the limitations that you are currently perceiving so that you can remember your Higher Self, your divine power and gifts, your Infinite Self and your Infinite capacity to choose and create.

Her work as an Intuitive Goddess coach involves helping women and sometimes men to cultivate their inner world so they can create their soul-aligned life with ease. She helps people create their soul-aligned life through coaching, quantum energy healing, DNA Activations, clearings and meditations.

Abigail works deeply and richly with the goddess in EVERY-thing she does. She inspires, activates and empowers you to step into your power to create the life you desire with ease and grace. She helps facilitate powerful transformation in her clients.

Through her work, her clients move from fear, disempowerment, disconnection, and confusion to experiencing clarity of vision and mission, motivated, empowered and a life where they really can have it ALL.

Connect with her at **www.moongoddessacademy.com**. You can also join her Facebook comunity, Moon Goddess Sacred Sanctum, at **www.facebook.com/groups/MoonGoddessSanctum**.

S. Pauline Michalovic

YES, MAGICA, YES! ∽

```
yes magIca yes
ageless tru joy,suspend tIme
 all thIngs possIble
```

INTENSIFYING

THANKFULNESS ∽

Abundance tonal
Amplify reality
Thanking creator

Blessing of Gaia
Intensifying thankful
Open vessel field

Extending vastness
Tru the petals beloved
High hertz frequency

PEACOCK ALCHEMY ~

beauty, transformation, strength
persistent patience

infinity heart
toroidal catalyst wise
heart emanation

alchemy wisdom
whole design strategy
we have been gifted

we are one, resound
creator and creation
one tone reverbs

under and over
tones resounding from the source
same moment, day, night

natural resource
symbolic of more essence
unity in source

speak as a crystal
creation transformer
wisdom in center

infinity toroidal
breath and water resonant
expose alignment

STILL POINT ⌇

still point
sensitivity exquisite
funnel of light
entrance to surrender
learning, remembering, teaching
chalice of the heart
all channels awake
I am the veil
the scent of roses
bring you to me
dancing your alter
feeling gnosis
as a spark comes
lofting on the breeze
ancient tones bringing truth wisdom
the vessel
the veil
lightening strikes
shining star pulsing
flower of life frequency
electric

EXHALE ON THE WANE ⤳

moon void of course,
death queen calls
she beckons, let go

nourish the release
green and brown rich life soil
soul compost divine

PRANIC DREAMS ∾

heart chant
fills chalice
vibration expands
offered to the ultimate beloved
creator, creation
most tender of hearts nourished w devotion
sustained tone, chalice filled
exhale blowing stardust across the universe
rain drops moon drops
pranic dreams
m a n i f e s t

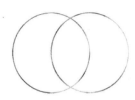

ABOUT THE AUTHOR
S. Pauline Michalovic

S. Pauline Michalovic is a holistic health practitioner, researcher and visionary, gracefully integrating thirty years of practice. Pauline is nationally certified and state licensed in massage therapy, contemporary cupping methods, visceral manipulation, and cranial sacral therapy. She is a yoga teacher, priestess initiate, sixth generation Reiki master, personal trainer, raw and whole foods chef. A remarkable western Renaissance woman, traditional and contemporary medicine woman, master massage therapist, nutrition and detox consultant, Pauline offers unique perspective to transformational wellness in Cortez, Colorado under the gaze of Mesa Verde National Park. As a healing emissary, Pauline joyously celebrates the divine spark at Mesa Verde Morning Sun, ecco bella organique: spa, retreat and private practice, resting in the beautiful and sacred four corners region of Southwest Colorado.

Yogic in creation, Pauline's vision Miraclewrx nourishes, educates and shares in the facilitation of universal healing, from the ion onward. Offering cutting edge innovative health care perspective, Miraclewrx, "Guardian of Life", gifts all health conditions and modalities positive therapeutic adjunct, including: Western, Eastern, traditional, contemporary, allopathic and holistic practices, gifting a layperson's "medicine for the people". Mesa Verde Morning Sun, home to Miraclewrx, specializes in oils, analgesics, essential oils, medicinal baths, oxygen therapies, detoxification and organic lifestyle. Pauline's professional and personal experience have led her to create The Guardian of Life model, a unified, comprehensive and highly integrated approach to the divine spark and biomechanics of health and wholeness. The Guardian of Life empowers health through simple and observable laws of nature. Pauline has studied at the University of Colorado, Colorado School of Healing Arts, Yoga Institute of Houston, International Cupping Therapy Association, The Barrell Institute, Upledger Institute, West Winds Academy of Massage Therapy, 13 Moon Mystery School, with affiliations including U.S. Olympic Diving, U.S. World Mountain Bike, and U.S. Freestyle Skiing. Pauline holds World and National titles in telemark skiing. Pauline's art and photography graces the insides of this book. To learn more... **infinitehealth@miraclewrx.com**

Special thanks to S. Pauline Michalovic for the use of her beautiful photography and artwork on the cover and through the pages of this book ~ much gratitude!

Catalina Rivera Dois

CHALICE SONG

Empty
and silent I wait
for you

Lovingly holding this space
for you

Expansive and still.
Calm at your will.

Mother I'm empty for you to fill
Mother I'm empty… empty… empty
Mother I'm empty for you to fill

In stillness I amplify
what rises from womb's dark sky
Sounding again and again and again:

A ripple of love like a singing wren
A ripple of Mother, for sisters and brothers
A ripple of love like a singing wren.

REMEMBERING OUR BODY TEMPLE ⌒

Listen love,
listen,
your cells and your atoms and soul
call out to you
again and again and again:

"As long as our body is not loved, trusted, and honored
as the sacred temple,
our Essence cannot fully reside on Earth."

It is time, it is time, it is time.

It is time my love, to reclaim your divine, wild, sensual innocence.

To reclaim the power and brilliance of your body temple
to light and fuel its magnetic flame,
that it may pull your essence from the Great Above to the Great Below,
right here where it is needed.

Like a lover calling in the night,
(enraptured, ecstatic longing)
allow your body to sing your essence home
that they may merge in magnificent waves of ecstasy,
the birthing of a star radiating light onto this plane
divine light,
here,
now,
fully embodied in Love.

Awaken and shed the chains of shame,
the layers of guilt,
the weight of pain and wounding held in your body
from this lifetime
from past lifetimes

from your personal story
and with a sigh of relief,
release the collective pain you've been holding for the One.

Yes, beloved!
Shed!
Shed and release it all!

Invoking the power of the earthquake to shake your very foundations
Invoking the volcanic eruption that has been building for centuries
Invoking the liquid heat and the wildfire of lava
burning it all to ashes
ashes rich with the radiant possibilities of the phoenix's rising.

It is time, it is time, it is time.
To burn in radiance, to fully arrive, to come home
to reclaim our holy wild sensual innocence, in body
in body…

Will you come?
Will you burn?
Will you light the way?

Divine Holy Shrine,
Beloved,
trusted,
honored.

Ecstasy's delight,
take flight, take flight

Take flight in ecstasy's delight.

(Archetype: Primal Goddess)

~MOON BLOOD~

From a time beyond time
and a place beyond space
I see women of radiant grace
Each of beauty and strength,
wise, true, tender, I face
lineage bearers of Mother's Embrace

Each a pearl in a strand, silver threaded in red
each one lovingly passing the cup
of red ruby light, condensed into matter,
Her force sung into sacred life water

Drops of light, drops of life, drops of blood
held in warmth and a loving embrace
in the void of the Mother,
in our own pelvic bowl
Love remember!
Pure magic we hold.

Remember this power inside you,
encoded to create and sustain,
flowing each moon, like a river of love:
Will you honor me now?
Once again?

Will you use me as Goddess intended,
to nourish the Earth and its life?

Will you use me as Goddess intended,
to birth and your essence midwife?

Will you use me as Goddess intended,
in magic and ritual with joy,
to create here a world of Her beauty,
of love and embracing of All?

I am here, as I always have been
waiting for you to awake

to the kiss of my ruby red droplets
on your thighs, on your lips,
feel me quake
Let me flow through your womb and your moon blood
Take me in as your sacrament once more
Let my magic run wild through your presence
Re-birthing your essence to soar

I am here, I am here, my beloved
Remember, remember, blood sings
Take me in,
with intent, love and reverence.
Let my pure magic begin

Igniting your throat with my power,
bursting open your heart with my love
settling deep in your belly and womb like a flood,
stoking fires in your passionate blood.

Into lava that flows into rivers
into rivers of radiant light,
expanding in waves of honey delight,
starburst reaching far! Far!
Beyond sight

I choose to remember, my sister,
To hold this moon cup once again,
to stand as a pearl on this ruby red thread.
Will you join this remembrance and spread?

Spread moon blood's sacred nature as sacrament,
as light of creation and more,
Will you join me as we starburst in radiance?
In ecstatic delight, Yes!
We soar!

(Archetype: Great Mother)

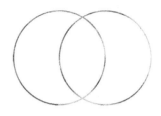

ABOUT THE AUTHOR

Catalina Rivera Dois

Catalina Rivera Dois is an awakening womb priestess and Keeper of Our Blood Mysteries Temple: a sacred space dedicated to the joyful remembrance and rebirthing of our blood mysteries into modern day life. She is an emissary of Mother's Love through simple heart/womb knowing, woman's magic and fun. Catalina is also a Reiki Master therapist and teacher, women's circles facilitator, self-retired labor & delivery room nurse, wife and loving mother of two.

Connect with Catalina at **www.catalinarivera.com.**

Janice Sapphire

MAKING LOVE TO MY LIFE ~

I drop into my womb space:
where the cancer is
where the cosmos is

Am I ready to come out of hiding?
My soul says yes.

I am quiet, the goddess springs from silence.

I am coming out of hiding so I can rebirth:
Transmute the cellular memories
My mother's imprinting
The great mother wound
carried in my womb.

Waking after surgery
I hear the voices of angels:

"Make love to your life."
Be a vessel for the earth angel
you are.

I feel Her love enter into me
and my blood filled with
Her Presence.

She is loving me in softness,
giving me peace and strength.
This is my path now:

Making love to my life.

THE PRAYER

I pray to the Love Voice in me
as Her vessel of light.

I stand as water:
it washes me, a
channel of the Holy Mother's elements.

Water:
cleanse me of all I fear and feel in fear.

I feel peace, power

My body:
an empty vessel to receive Her.

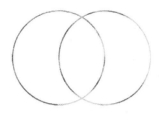

ABOUT THE AUTHOR

Janice Sapphire

Janice Sapphire is a Priestess Initiate of the 13 Moon Mystery School since 2015 and celebrates her 5th year in the study of Priestessing in a Temple of Sisters from all over the world. She is an active everyday Priestess in all areas of her life.

Janice has overcome uterine and endometrial cancer since the writing of this essay in December 2017. Today, she is thriving and continues to "Make Love to Her Life" while sharing her wisdom and insights with an abundance of clients in the United States and Internationally.

Janice is an intuitive healer and angelic medium with a great understanding of the energetic healing associated with the physical, mental, and emotional components. At age 13, Janice was introduced to Unity/Science of Mind Church metaphysical healing and mind/body connections to God. The Goddess call came along with her Shaman path as an intuitive healer. Celtic ancestory awakened in the gene codes within her. Janice has witnessed incredible and profound spiritual healing in her own life and in the lives of her clients and students. She can easily navigate through multiple dimensions while observing the energy and story of her clients, zooming right into the gem with her Horus- and hawk-like insight. As a professional Intuitive Spiritual Life Coach, and with healing touch as a CA state massage therapist, Janice's gifts have helped many people unblock, change patterns, and open up the path to receiving and manifesting their dreams.

Janice lives in California on the beautiful central coast. Visit her at **www.divinewellbeingmastery. com** for more powerful metaphysical tools to clear energy and feel the magic that lives inside of you.

Jacquie Eva Rose Shenton

I SEE YOU, BEAUTIFUL

I see you, beautiful:

The woman you are, the woman you will become

Your journey to wholeness already complete,
already begun

The depths of the oceans already searched
—all you have been through in the name of my love.

The tides rise
and fall,

guiding you Home now

More whole, more beautiful
than ever before

Left: Art by Jacquie Eva Rose Shenton

OM MANI
PADME
HUM

Left & right pages: Art by Jacquie Eva Rose Shenton

~THE INITIATOR~

I am
the Initiator
I set fire in your bones!

I am the clarifier of truth

I am justice as she prevails over you
with the translucent spear of love

Give yourself to me for I hold the keys to your
awakening.

I am honour
as she prevails in you at this time

I am right action,
knowing whatever consequences fall from truth
benefit the whole

I am the morning star of the lost self,
who finds her way here by facing the shadow
in complete love and emptiness

Empty vessel:
Be with me.

I will open the gate of your love
so that the ocean of truth streams
from your hips
    your eyes
        your tongue

In honour of all those who have been before
and who will come again to drink from my waters of
truth:
Will you let me in?

Let me rise up through you
and wash away all that no longer fits

The cosmos is around you and through you—
There is nowhere I will not enter.

I am forever in you and with you
Let your gate open now....

Hail and welcome!

Right: Art by Jacquie Eva Rose Shenton

THE QUEEN OF DEATH ⤳

In the dark hollow
I hear you, oh Queen.
In the bowels of the earth
you breathe to me: e n t e r...

In the dark spaces
I reach for you:
Trusting
Touching

Holding your cold hand
allowing you to guide me.

Moving deeper with you now
I embrace your mysteries:
Sinking into your spaces
I fall and surrender

Curled up with you
in this lost nest
Breathing
Becoming
Dying

All that is left is to let go
All that is left is to let go

Emptiness
Stillness

In this moment
it is done

Right: Art by Jacquie Eva Rose Shenton

DEVELOPING HER WORK

PAIN-MY TEACHER

I approach you, pain.

You are teaching me with your burning persistence
You are showing me with your vice grip
How to feel:

Presence
Gravity
This plane
Here
Now.

I feel your presence over and over again.

I breathe you.
I breathe your roaring insistence
to be felt NOW—
RIGHT NOW

I feel your snake energy seeking
the way up

I meet your snake energy shaking
my body to the core

I meet you in darkness
and at the height of full moon.

Each time you come, you dig deeper
Demanding to be felt.

Hour by hour
Moment by moment
Second by second
I meet you

My dark beloved
My teacher.

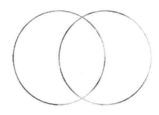

ABOUT THE AUTHOR

Jacquie Eva Rose Shenton

Jacquie Eva Rose Shenton is a fifth year initiate of Priestess Presence. A committed and dedicated sister of the temple. A highly intuitive, creative, vulnerable and humble human being, she is an inspired activist for catalysing change within the self and others. Here on this earth with a deep purpose to unite the masculine and feminine within and really understand the core concept of self love, Jacquie is an awakening midwife who loves supporting others to step into and own their personal power.

Jacquie's radiates Muse, Priestess & Alchemical Goddess energy. She is a good listener and guide. Her strongest gifts are transforming poison into medicine, the ability to deep dive into the realms of unconsciousness to bring back the gems buried there and holding space for others to do the same. Connect with her at: **www.harmoniousbeing.co.uk**

Deborah Wood

OUT OF HIDING

What do I need to lay down
to cross this gateway?

Speak the truth.

What's real
lies in the deep darkness
beneath.

Go there—
Dive deep—go
through the gateway—reap.

You must
be crazy, ME
Write? Transmit? Mother?

I have nothing to say.
I hide. That's what I do.
I'm the silent one.

Flesh out
the wound sore.
Live life waited for.

I want to run.
Delete.
Brush off, walk away.
Priestess presence—not today.

But wait—
The sarcophagus.
Breath slowly...deeply.
Isis the initiator.

It's not what you thought.
The initiation is bigger than
your tiny little dream.

Remember who you are.
You are a Star.

She's unveiling you. Showing you off.
Her daughter beautiful, bright
Who has something to say.

Yes, it's all been said before.
But not the way you can deliver it.

Your journey is unique
and you've done it in beauty and grace.

Faith, my love.
With the Divine on your side
there's no need to hide.

Heal the wound:
the sisterhood wound, the brotherhood wound.
The wound of separation.

Okay I say…

I go to the forest and speak:
Trees, hear this: She wants me to write.
Not just journal—but write for The One.
She wants me to be seen.

I entrain the forest: will you speak through me?
Lady of Communion: will you speak through me?

Beauty: will you speak through me?

Sitting with my back to Cedar,
I entwine with trees, plants, insects, the forest floor.

Eyes up in awe
golden sunlight through maple leaves
curves of cedar branches.
Green and gold.

What's being asked of you is to be yourself.
Your true essence, soul star, light beam of Mother.

I lay in the dark in faith.
I release, I trust.
I ask Her, 'How do I hide?'

You hide behind your hair
your weight
your kids
your husband
your job.
You hide from your fear.

You've hidden for so long you have forgotten
who you are and where you came from.

I come from Fire and Water and Moon

I Am Dancing Flame Moonwater:
Mother's Daughter

Rebirth, resurrection, Phoenix

I am out of hiding—

Move me!

~ISIS~

The key: geometry, sacred shape luminaries
—an open channel, bright.

Drop in. Feel all of it.
Become it.

Third eye spins.
Light body is
shapeshifter of sacred frequency
—transmuter, merging love light into the wound energy:
dissolution of delusion
Fluid, etherical, thick, dark.

Love comes in the frequency to match what
needs alchemizing.

Color
Sound
Form:
Isis
I-sis
Is-is
I-sssss

Infinity, swirling white on white:
merging, alchemizing, dissolving
all that appears as anxiety, control, anger,
wiping it clear, with pure Love.

Black on black, velvety enfoldment
oozing oil,
deep, dark Love
covering, softening, steeping
healing hidden shame-filled wounds: infected.

Umbra solis

Clarity of illusions and truth:
I see. I feel. I know. I love.
I am whole.

You are whole.

ORACLE

Moon light orb
Dancing light   moving
in sacred forms and frequencies:

Milky golden blue
        pink green white
Changing transmuting

Love!
New!

I am new. Renewed
Wholeness rising from doubt

Wings of light
Paper thin, translucent

Light body activated
Winged one alight

Tongue activated,
tasting then sucking in nectar
of flowers from the sun

Turning amrita into words of life.

∽MOON GODDESS∾

I open
and speak through my hands:
Healing
Writing

Open lotus mudra at my throat

Dancing flame mudra under full moon,
clear sky, dark

Speaking to the land and trees
Rooting my feet in the earth.

Creating space to be
So I can go do priestessing:

Write with Her voice
Embody Her heart
Move from Her mind

Blessed hands, worthy hands, Sacred Mother's hands

Sitting on the front step
gazing at the moon two days from her fullness:

Wispy clouds breeze across Her face
A halo of gold and white forms around Her,
then becomes a rainbow-hued halo.

Alchemical Goddess Moon!

Imprint this image on my heart, mind, womb
I am She...She is Me

Isis
Moon Goddess
Dancing-flame Moon Goddess.

~ SACRED UNION MUDRA ~

Palms face one another,
arms width apart

Bow and wave to one another:
coming closer in the dance

Energies colliding—swirling
in the e-motion—

Settling in a merge...

Magnetic friction forming
a ball of coherent energy:
turning, rising,
falling

as one united
yet apart.

Two become one
become three:
Co-creating a new story.

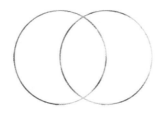

ABOUT THE AUTHOR

Deborah Wood

Deborah Wood: I am a massage therapist passionate about my calling. I combine energy healing techniques and craniosacral therapy into my massage with the intent to bring balance and restoration on a deeper soul level.

As I am in a state of complete acceptance I invite you to open up to the Divine Love that is channeled through the portal of my open heart and hands, guiding your soul body to its desired state of coherence. In a place of empty presence I feel in-tuitively facilitating your work.

Connect with me at **www.empowerreclaim.com.**

Connect at
www.PriestessPresence.com